MW01284298

Linda —

Your a giant spirit! But more growth is coming! The word "exponetial growth" I hear exponetial, "exponetial growth".

— Strength to your expansion

— Wally 4/6/23

Cover art by: <u>Mariah Diamond Johnson</u>

The Benefits of Speaking in Tongues
(A 31 Day Devotional)

Author: New Mystic

Other Titles Available by New Mystic:

1. *"An Introduction to the Seven Spirits of God"*
2. *"The Spiritual Dynamics of Hand Drumming"*
3. *"A Mystical Introduction to Angels"*
4. *"The Stars Deserve a Second Look"*
5. *"Engaging the King"*

© Copyright May 17, 2019
All rights reserved. This book is protected by the copyright laws of the United States of America. This book may not be copied or reprinted for commercial gain or profit. The use of short quotations or occasional page copying for personal or group study is permitted and encouraged. Permission will be granted upon request.

Unless otherwise identified, scripture quotations are from the New King James Version (**NKJV**) ®. Copyright © 1982 by Thomas Nelson, Inc. Used by permission. All rights reserved. Most scripture quotations unmarked (example **John 3:3**) are taken from the Amplified ® Bible Classic (**AMPC**), Copyright © 1954, 1958, 1962, 1964, 1965, 1987 by the Lockman Foundation.
Scriptures marked (**NIV)** are taken from the HOLY BIBLE, NEW INTERNATIONAL VERSION®, Copyright 1973, 1978, 1984 International Bible Society. Scriptures marked (**YLT**) are taken from Young's Literal Translation of the Holy Bible by Robert Young, Copyright 1862. Scriptures marked (**AENT**) are taken from Aramaic English New Testament, Copyright 2012. Scriptures marked (**MIRROR**) are taken from The Mirror translation, Copyright 2014.

Any 'emphasis' within Scriptures is the author's own.

For books and other resources go to:
http://www.newmystic.net/

For audio resources go to:
http://new-mystic.podomatic.com/

Download the free app @ Apple store or Google play:
Ekklessia Uprising

Table of Contents

Dedication

This book is dedicated to those who are on the journey to sonship.

This is for you!

Bereishit

I wonder when the idea was birthed to have divinity dwell within humanity? Before the beginning (Hebrew: bereishit), did the Son volunteer the Spirit; did they draw straws; did they vote? Selah

Maybe I did jump the gun, let's start from **my beginning**. In the early 80s during summer break, I returned from Oklahoma University, college, to Ft. Leavenworth, a military base in Kansas, where my father was stationed.

I didn't look forward to off-season football training in the Kansas heat. Yet, I was looking forward to getting back to attending the *youth bible study that I attended on Sunday and Wednesday nights whenever I was in town.

I believe the first meeting of the summer was a Sunday night. The meeting was going as usual until prayer time. I love this part of the gathering. It was a good prayer meeting if one or both legs fell asleep. Anyway, I found my piece of carpet and 'assumed the position' then I heard something odd. To hear better, I opened one eye.

As soon as we were done, my hand shot up, and I said, "WHAT WAS BOBBY DOING?". My Bible study leader responded, "That's speaking in tongues." I said, "What?" He said, "Speaking in tongues". I said, "Is it good or bad?". He said, "Good". I crossed the room, stood in front of him, and said, "Well then I WANT IT! What do I do?" He showed me some scriptures:

Acts 1: 8	1 Corinthians 14:4
Acts 2: 1-21	Romans 8:26
Acts 10:44-47	Jude 20
Acts 19:1-7	

I read the scriptures and then he led me in a prayer to receive the Baptism of the Holy Spirit. I prayed the prayer out loud. I expected a 'force' to open my mouth and make a foreign language (an unknown tongue) burst out. In anticipation of the 'force', I shut my mouth and bit down hard. After all that, no new prayer language. I was disappointed. I was then told that if you prayed the prayer that I was filled with the Holy Spirit and later the prayer language (new tongues) would come. I was encouraged to believe and "wait on the Lord". I believed but I was not sure what "wait on the Lord" meant. As I waited, weeks passed and others in the group got their prayer language.

I waited then 'new' people (recently saved from the streets) got their prayer language. I stop believing and started reasoning & judging. I thought, "That's not fair, I've been a Christian longer than them and they don't even know the Bible as much as me..."

Time passed, and only me & one girl had not received. There had to be a reason, so I created one.

Obviously, she and I were chosen NOT to speak in tongues. We were chosen to be "a bridge" between our "tongue-talking-group" and the rest of the world. Yes, we were special too. We were now ambassadors on behalf of the group. I felt much better about myself as I attended next week's bible study. It seemed that balance had been restored; "everybody was special; everybody had a role".

Then one Sunday afternoon, my parents dropped me off a little early to the Bible study. I met the Bible teacher in the front yard. We talked about the week. Our chat was interrupted by a girl running towards us screaming, "I can do it, I can do it, I can do it..." I knew that girl. She was the other ambassador. I started screaming, "**Nooooo, Nooooo, I'm alone!**"

We both continued to scream until she stood before us. The bible teacher smiled at her and turned to comfort me by saying, "Let's pray". I thought, "easy for him to say since they could 'do it". I was now the only one in the group that couldn't. What a horrible moment in time. They prayed; I folded my arms and watched them in disgust.

"Wait a minute."

"Hold the fort."
I stared as the two prayed; I saw something.
They opened their mouths.
They moved their mouths.
I could see the tongue in their mouth move.
I was amazed.
You see, every time I went to pray in tongues – I would shut my mouth.
They opened their mouths
Could it be this simple?
Just allow the Holy Spirit to use my mouth, my tongue, my breath?
Just yield?

O.M.G. (Oh My God)

I ran into the house, called my parents to pick me up early.
I needed to try what I just saw.
My parents took their time.
I finally got home, went down to my room in the basement.
Time to try again.

OMG

Guess who was no longer an ambassador?
I spoke in tongues in my basement.
I spoke in tongues at the Wednesday night bible study.
I later spoke in tongues at the Sunday night bible study.
I was now a part of the group.
++
P.S. Your invited to join the 'tongue talking' group too.
Follow these steps for a personal tongue talking emergence experience:

1. Go to a device (PC, Apple, smart phone…)
2. Enter my website: https://new-mystic.podomatic.com/
3. Download and Play this title:
    - "Speaking Tongues for Doers of the word"

***Note:** this is the same bible study where I heard my first angel story (see "A Mystical Introduction to Angels")

Preface

"Praying in tongues";
"praying in the (Holy) spirit";
Heavenly language;
"speaking in tongues"

– all these phrases will be used interchangeably throughout the book. Also, I will not be using the technical term, "glossolalia" in the devotional but, if you like it – you can add it.

This is a 31-day devotional to help believers (**NOT THINKERS**) keep their mind on the things above by utilizing the many benefits of speaking in tongues. With your mind being set or better said, "**continuously reset**" on the Lord Most High, you will achieve that which you were fashioned to do in your designated space-time.

This book is full of revelation, revealed mysteries, but they are powerless to transform unless acted on. Maybe I should make this a workbook and not a devotional? Or does 'devotion' require work? I believe the answer is "Yes". **Work motivated by love** will produce sweet devotion and a much-needed transfiguration!

1 Corinthians 13:1 (Mirror)
"Speaking in tongues is not the point; love is."

I've learned and still learning that Abba (Father God) is more interested in those devoted to Him (worshippers) and not so much with those working for acceptance or motivated by fear. A very effective way to keep oneself in the love of Abba is by speaking in tongues! One who speaks in tongues 'speaks to God'. God is Love. Therefore, he who speaks in tongues 'communicates to Love'! As often as you engage with LOVE- you cannot help but be transfigured by LOVE ❤

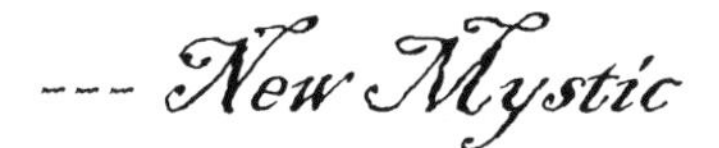

Introduction

Welcome to your devotional. The goal of this book is to motivate you to pray in tongues more, to increase your "tongue time". This devotional includes the many benefits of speaking in tongues. I personally don't do things because people tell me or because "I just should"; I NEED to know "WHY". There must be BENEFIT that's worth the investment of my time & energy. Keep reading and experience the benefits of speaking in tongues!

What if you don't speak in tongues? Keep reading, by the end of the book you will. Or you can ask the Holy Spirit right NOW, believe & receive and He will fill you! You will have at least two manifestations:

1. A clearer understanding of His written and spoken words;
2. A personal prayer language

What if you have been taught that "speaking in tongues is of the devil"? You are in the right place, I believe "**Day 1**" will address that. You will read about when I was confronted by a good friend with the exact same concern.

The book is set up as a daily devotional. According to Wikipedia, "Daily devotionals are publications which provide specific spiritual reading for each calendar day. Daily devotionals have a long tradition in religious communities, with the earliest known Christian example, "Gælic *Feliré",* written in Ireland in the Ninth Century. They tend to be associated with a daily time of prayer and meditation."

So, my 'specific spiritual reading' will contain (4) sections:

a. A Scripture(s)
b. A specific benefit of speaking in tongues
c. An anecdote or supporting story
d. Your Personal Thoughts/Revelation(s):

Also, each calendar day will have an area to document the results of your 'daily time of prayer (speaking in tongues) and meditation'.

You're not required to follow the days in sequence. You may wish to repeat the same day until the truth you read becomes ingrained in your soul.

You have a promise from Father God, that if you invest in spiritual things (aka spiritual readings) that you are GUARANTEED to receive directly from His Spirit!

Galatians 6:8,9 AMPC

[8] Whoever sows to please their flesh,
from the flesh will reap destruction;
whoever sows to please the Spirit,
from the Spirit will reap
eternal life.

[9] Let us not become weary in doing good,
for at the proper time
we will reap a harvest if
we do not give up.

Day 1

Reference: 1 Corinthians 14: 39(AMPC)

[39] So to conclude, my brethren, earnestly desire and set your hearts on prophesying (on being inspired to preach and teach and to interpret God's will and purpose), and **do not forbid or hinder speaking in unknown tongues**.

Benefit:

Speaking in tongues allows you to be biblical. You become a "doer of the word", since you are personally NOT 'forbidding or hindering' speaking in tongues. Plus, it allows you to 'do all things'; most people only do 'some things' or only 'a few things'. If you continue reading and being, you will be **un-hindering the speaking in unknown tongues!**

Anecdote:

I had a similar experience like what is written in Acts 19:1-6:

> *[1]While Apollos was in Corinth, Paul went through the upper inland districts and came down to Ephesus. There he found some disciples.*
>
> *[2] And he asked them, Did you receive the Holy Spirit when you believed [on Jesus as the Christ]? And they said, No, we have not even heard that there is a Holy Spirit.*
>
> *[3] And he asked, Into what [baptism] then were you baptized? They said, Into John's baptism.*
>
> *[4] And Paul said, John baptized with the baptism of repentance, continually telling the people that they should believe in the One Who was to come after him, that is, in Jesus [having a conviction full of joyful trust that He is Christ, the Messiah, and being obedient to Him].*

> [5] *On hearing this they were baptized [again, this time] in the name of the Lord Jesus.* [6] *And as Paul laid his hands upon them, the Holy Spirit came on them; and* ***they spoke in [foreign, unknown] tongues (languages)*** *and prophesied.*

My story did not occur in Ephesus but in a dorm room at the University of Oklahoma. I recall, I was studying in my room and there was a knock at my door. I went and opened the door and there stood my good friend. He said, I know you speak in tongues. I said to myself, "Hmmm". He went on to say, "Speaking of tongues is of the devil!". He closed the door. I sat in my chair. He continued, "I know this guy that met a girl that spoke in tongues. He spoke with her and then cast a devil out of her. And she didn't speak in tongues anymore. So, speaking in tongues is of the devil." I was still speechless but thinking to myself, "I don't know about that girl…" My friend took my silence as concurrence and pivoted and left my room. I returned to my homework. For some reason, his story didn't concern me. I think, I must have remembered and believed these verses:

> *"Which of you fathers, if your son asks for a fish, will give him a snake instead? Or if he asks for an egg, will him a scorpion? If you then, though you are evil, know how to give good gifts to your children, how much more will your Father in heaven give the Holy Spirit to those who ask Him!" (Luke 11:11-13)*

I don't know who the girl asked but I asked my Father in heaven for the Holy Spirit and I received. A few days later, my friend called and said, "You're right." I said, "Right about what?". He said, "You know, you are right!" I again said, "Right about what?" He said, "**Tongues are of God**!"

Your Personal Thoughts/Revelation(s):

Day 2

Reference: 1 Corinthians 14: 2 (AMPC)

[2] For one who speaks in an [unknown] tongue speaks not to men but to God, for no one understands *or* catches his meaning, because in the [Holy] Spirit he utters secret truths *and* hidden things [not obvious to the understanding].

Benefit:

One of the benefits of speaking in tongues is you get to by-pass "the line" and speak directly to the Source.

Anecdote:

You may have heard that communication is an art. Well speaking in tongues makes you a 'master communicator'. He who speaks in tongues speaks God's language in perfect dialect.

Speaking in tongues is "the secret" to perfect communication with the Living God. Speaking in tongues eliminates the fear of being misunderstood by authority, the Highest authority.

The more I speak in tongues; the more I speak to God. The more that I speak to God, the more comfortable I get with my God. My relationship with Him gets stronger. I believe, we all need to have STRONG relationships with God.
Speaking in tongues builds your relationship with Him in private so that you may be bold for Him in public.

I echo the Apostle Paul, "Finally, my brethren be STRONG in the Lord!

Your Personal Thoughts/Revelation(s):

Day 3

Reference: 1 Corinthians 14:2

[2]For one who speaks in an unknown tongue speaks not to men but to God, for no one understands or catches his meaning, because in the Holy Spirit he utters secret truths and hidden things not obvious to the understanding.

Benefit:

Speaking in tongues allows one to engage in His Kingdom as a citizen and as a son of the King. The central stabilizing component of every culture is language. A common language unifies a people.

Speaking in tongues unifies the people in His Kingdom; it is away to have the "mind of Christ". We are not only unified together but we are also unified with the King.

Anecdote:

Every child speaks the language of their Father! You are born of God thus be 'normal' and speak the language of God.

One Saturday on the way to my local fellowship in Washington DC. I was led by the Spirit to stop in a store. I was told, "You will have a better understanding of My Kingdom from this stop." I thought, "I don't think so but let's see." So, I stop at the store, Patriot Harley-Davidson. Yes, a motorcycle shop. I parked and entered into another kingdom. These people look different, acted different, and had their own common language. All thriving cultures are bonded language. Your invited to engage with His Heaven culture. I left with a new perspective of the heavenly Kingdom, the value of language, and purchased a bandana.

Your Personal Thoughts/Revelations:

Day 4

Reference: 1 Corinthians 14:4,5 AMP
[4] He who speaks in a [strange] tongue edifies *and* improves himself…
[5] Now I wish that you might all speak in tongues…

Benefit:

If you speak in tongues, you become **strong** in spirit. If speak in tongues "a lot", you become **mighty** in spirit. If you become fluent, then you become **more** in spirit.

Anecdote:

This is the first benefit that I experienced and continue to experience. In tandem with Ruach (Spirit of God), speaking in tongues is what spinach is to Popeye – it makes a natural man become a Full Spiritual Man (F.S.M.)!

Enoch became a FSM by inputs from Grandfather Adam and walking with God. We can walk with God via our vibrant tongue talking life.

I'm becoming the man my Father has designed me to be.

1 Corinthians 14:18
I thank God that I speak in [strange] **tongues** (languages) **more than any of you *or* all of you put together**;

As you continue the process, you are the one; Our Father has designed.

Your Personal Thoughts/Revelations:

Day 5

Reference: 1 Corinthians 14: 4 (AMPC)

[4]He who speaks in a strange tongue edifies and improves himself...

Benefit:

Another benefit of speaking in tongues is it illuminates and prepares your inner man for alterations and modifications. Your inner man has at least (8) spirit gateways:

1. Revelation
2. Intuition
3. Lover of your Soul (aka Fear of God)
4. Prayer
5. Reverence
6. Faith
7. Hope
8. Worship

Anecdote:

Your speaking in tongues prepares your house for edification. Speaking in tongues gives permission to the King of Glory to perfect you.

> **Philippians 1:6**
> And I am convinced and sure of this very thing, that **He Who began a good work in you will continue** until the day of Jesus Christ [right up to the time of His return], developing [that good work] and perfecting and bringing it to full completion **in you.**

We allow the King of Glory (Psalm 24) to enter through these gates. While speaking in tongues, you partner with the King of Glory. We are allowing the glory of God (His Glory, His Life) to flow in our spirit and through these gateways. This 'flowing' allows the King to come through our gates. He begins using us for His glory. The flow of glory impacts spirit (first), then soul, then your body. A good book for reference on your gates is called the "Gateways of the three-fold nature of man" by Ian Clayton. I read the book and it took me about 50 hours to address my gates. I started with my "first love gate", then my spirit gates, then my soul gates, and lastly my body gates. Once I did, I became a more useful vessel for my King.

Psalm 24:6-8

[6]This is the generation of those who seek Him, who seek Your face, O God of Jacob. Selah
[7]Lift up your heads, O you gates; and be lifted up, you age-abiding doors, that the King of glory may come in.
[8]Who is the King of glory? The Lord strong and mighty, the Lord mighty in battle.

Years before learning about my gates, I would spend time, concentrated time speaking in tongues. The times I would choose would be after studying copious hours for college finals or during long road trips. When finals were over, I would rent a hotel room, unplug the phone & TV and engage in hours upon hours of speaking in tongues. I recommend that you find opportunities to pray in tongues in "multi-hour" packets. I know from experience that frequent speaking in tongues gives one a "3-fold makeover!"

Enjoy you make-over!

Your Personal Thoughts/Revelations:

Day 6

Reference:

Jude 20 AMPC
[20]But you, beloved, build yourselves up [founded] on your most holy faith, praying in the Holy Spirit

Benefit:

Speaking in tongues can and will build up your (vital) faith.

Anecdote:

The bible says, "we live by faith" (Romans 1:17). Faith is critical to your successful life on earth and every other realm. Frequent speaking in tongues will help you live this life as a maturing son of God. God has a plan for your life. Faith helps you follow that divinely crafted plan.

When I'm at a crossroads or in doubt; I speak in tongues. This devotional recommends that speaking in tongues becomes a lifestyle and not an emergency plan. Praying in tongues does not remove obstacles; it makes one ABLE to break through all obstacles and any barriers.

Yes, speaking in tongues will cause you to realize that a mature son of God is **unstoppable**. You need to be confident in who you are in Him.

You need to be a confident tongue-talking new creature!

Speak On !!!

Your Personal Thoughts/Revelations:

Day 7

Reference:

Jude 21 AMPC
[21]Guard and keep yourselves in the love of God; expect and patiently wait for the mercy of our Lord Jesus Christ which will bring you unto life eternal.

Benefits:

Speaking in tongues triggers Love in you and out of you!

Also, speaking in tongues supports the bonding of host and the Divine.

Anecdote:

God is Love. Also, the most powerful force in the omni-universe is love. Faith works by love. Love never fails. Forget a lucky charm, **love will motivate you to greatness** (if you let it).

When I first saw Heidi Baker at conference in Washington, DC, my definition for love got extremely updated. She shared (3) stories from her mission in Africa that were beyond amazing. So, during my ushering, I repented of my 'baby understanding of love'.
I knew many, miracle stories surrounded Heidi. For years, I had been hoping to add more stories to my portfolio. After she spoke, I had a vision. I saw, "*a Huge (love) Pipe, a conduit. In this pipe, faith flowed like millions of gallons oil".* According to this vision, this faith was the foundation of all her miracles. I felt that my Father in heaven had revealed the secret of Galatians 5:6, "how faith works by love!" I was grateful for the revelation. I was so excited, I asked the Lord to show me my

pipe. We all want answered prayer but sometimes... Anyway, He showed me my pipe. Have you ever seen a "pin prick"? Well, I could barely see light through my pipe. A tear rolled down my cheek.

I felt like the lady with the issue of blood. "If only I could touch Heidi, my (love) pipe could grow, faith would flow, and miracles would abound..." That should be easy, as an usher I had access to guest speakers – I will just go up front and get her to lay hands on me. I opened my eyes and looked toward the stage. All routes toward Heidi were blocked by prostrate bodies. (Oh no.)

I felt hopeless and empty of love. I bowed my head. I mouthed a repentance prayer and quietly spoke in tongues.

I thought, "Maybe someday I could grow my pipe or ..." Another tear hit my cheek. Eyes still shut, I stood there consoling myself.

After more tears, I felt a hand on my heart and heard a woman's prayer. I looked down and it was Heidi Baker laying hands on me. I was shocked and speechless.

The Lord made a way out of no way. I knew hope. I, like the lady of the issue of blood, knew by faith that I was healed. My heart was alive; my pipe had promise: and I was on the journey entering into **"peace (untroubled, undisturbed well-being."**.

Luke 8:48

48 And He said to her, your faith has made you well! Go (enter) into peace (untroubled, undisturbed well-being).

Your Personal Thoughts/Revelations:

Day 8

Reference: 1 Corinthians 14:2 KJV

[2]... for no man understandeth him; howbeit in the spirit he speaketh mysteries.

Benefit:

Speaking in tongues causes the brain to become familiar with mysteries.

Speaking in tongues opens the mind to mysteries.

Anecdote:

The Kingdom is a mystery; Mystery is our native environment.

There is something about the human condition that makes us comfortable with the familiar; the status quo; comfortable with normal. I believe "normal is over rated"!

During a vision, I saw myself in an apartment. To my surprise, everything was in its place. The carpet had no clutter. The kitchen counters were clean. The kitchen sink was empty. In the sitting area, there was a chair, a couch, a table, and a tall 6-shelf book case. The apartment seemed to be mine. In the natural, my apartment looks "well lived in"; aka messy. It was rarely ready for guests or entertaining. As I walked around, it was obvious I had spent a lot of effort to make the place presentable. I heard a knock at the door. I went to the door and looked through the peep hole. I saw Jesus standing at my door knocking. In that moment, I recalled that He had come several times before. And in those previous encounters, I had not opened the door and let him into my messy apartment.

Well it was a new day; the apartment was presentable. I opened the door. I was finally proud enough to show Him around my apartment. I began the tour. I led Him around and highlighted my cleanliness, but He walked away from my presentable sitting area towards the brick wall on the other-side of the room. As he turned away, I said, "Look there's even room for dancing". I thought He would be impressed with the space I made for dancing and worship. He did not pause to look or even acknowledge my statement. He stood before the empty brick wall and pointed at the middle of the wall. I thought, "Man I knew I should had placed a poster or painting there." After my thought, He took His finger and plunked a hole in my wall. It looked like 2 or 3 bricks were gone. Jesus is powerful! I guess, "He didn't want a picture here but a window". This whole time, He has not spoken; I have. He motions to me to look through the hole. I approached the site of my future window and looked.

I saw, "Stars, multitudes of stars, and more stars..." I stepped back from the hole and He said, **"Do you want to go there or stay here?"** I was not expecting that. I thought the goal was to have a "presentable apartment". Plus, I could not see 'there'. The location, 'there', was a mystery. I clearly heard the question, but my brain did not understand. My brain was incapable of understanding the mystery.

The apartment represented my life. Speaking in tongues will prepare you (your life) for visitation. Speaking in tongues will position you to go further than your 'unconditioned' brain will allow you to go.

Do you want to go there or stay here?

<u>Amos 3:3 NKJV</u>
"Can two walk together, unless they are agreed?"

Another benefit of speaking in tongues is the revealing the mystery of Fatherhood. Speaking in tongues allows you and the Father the ability to be "agreement"; the ability to walk together as a Father and son! This is the relationship that Yeshua came to initiate!

<u>2 Corinthians 6:18 AMPC</u>
[18]And I will be a Father to you, and you shall be My sons and daughters, says the Lord Almighty.

Union is the Prime Objective.

Your Personal Thoughts/Revelations:

Day 9

Reference:

1 Corinthians 14:14
For if I pray in an unknown tongue, my spirit prays, but my mind is unproductive.

Benefit:

He, who speaks in tongues, conditions his mind as a King.

Anecdote:

He who speaks in tongues rewires his or her brain. I call it, "kingdom brain conditioning". (Note: there many chemical ways to rewire the brain; none of which I recommend.)

I was watching the 2016 movie, "Arrival". I will try not to spoil the movie for you and do recommend seeing it. [Note to self: create a list of recommended movies]

Anyway, in a dialogue between the main two characters they discussed this term, "**Sapir-Whorf hypothesis**". In the first 2 or 3 viewings, the term just went over my head and into the movie audio background. I felt led to see if this hypothesis was real or just movie fantasy. In my research, I found another benefit to speaking in tongues.

The Google definition of the hypothesis, Sapir-Whorf, is *a theory developed by Edward* **Sapir** *and Benjamin Lee* **Whorf** *that states that an individual's thoughts and actions are determined by the language or languages that individual speaks.*

So, I dare you to follow this: a 2016 movie used a 1929 theory to become the its foundation so that this 'Day's benefit' would be available in a 2019 devotional!

Are you still with me? I bet you want to see the movie now. I found out the hypothesis actually existed in the real world and I give kudos to the movie producer for being a deep thinker. Then, I thought, "Are my thoughts and actions being determined by the (unknown) languages that I speak?" According to the Sapir-Whorf hypothesis and my own experiences, the answer is YES!

Are YOUR thoughts and actions being determined by the unknown languages (speaking in tongues) that you speak?

You will find out if you stay on the journey – feel free to capture your personal observations in the back of this book. Once, your test is complete – please contact me – I'm sure it would be a great interview!

Please read this article "**Does the Linguistic Theory at the Center of the Film 'Arrival' Have Any Merit?**" You can read it here or type the article name into your computer search engine.

> *"Working to decode this mysterious language, accomplished human linguist Louise Banks—played in the sci-fi film Arrival by actress Amy Adams—begins to have visions of the past and future as her perception of time shifts from linear to circular. In other words, thinking in a different language causes her thought patterns to change. This is a core idea at the heart of the film: that an intimate relationship exists between the language you speak and the way you perceive the world.*

*The idea that "there's a link between the shape of language and what people actually talk about," actually has roots in 20th century linguistics theory, says Ives Goddard, a curator and linguist in the National Museum of Natural History's Department of Anthropology. Known as the **"Sapir-Whorf hypothesis,"** this theory states that language doesn't just give people a way to express their thoughts—it influences or even determines those thoughts. On the flip side, the evolution of a language is shaped by the culture and environment its speakers live in.*

http://www.smithsonianmag.com/science-nature/does-century-old-linguistic-hypothesis-center-film-arrival-have-any-merit-180961284/

Your Personal Thoughts/Revelations:

Day 10

Reference: Galatians 6:10 AMPC

[10] So then, as occasion *and* opportunity open up to us, let us do good to all people [not only being useful or profitable to them, but also doing what is for their spiritual good and advantage]. Be mindful to be a blessing, especially to those of the household of faith [those who belong to God's family with you, the believers].

Benefit:

When you choose to speak in tongues, you create 'the occasion' and you open opportunities for you and others to be a blessing.

Anecdote:

Speaking tongues always provides "opportunity". Like training in a gym lifting weights, speaking in tongues is training for your 'spiritual muscles'. If your muscles are fit/strong, then you can be a blessing to the 'weak'.

I was recently (March 2019) in a meeting. After speaking in tongues in and with the group, I had a vision. My speaking in tongues opened an opportunity aka a vision. [Note: a vision received, shared, and acted on becomes a blessing.]

The vision:
"I saw a large stadium. The stadium was mostly filled with believers. The believers were focused on the 3 Figures in the center of the field. These were not ordinary 'celebrities'; They were the Godhead, the Trinity!!!

The crowd knew who they were worshipping. The crowd was fully engaged. The Trinity was doing a 'circular' dance (Hebrew: *Machowl*). It seemed to me to that was the perfect environment – Creator & Creation together in one place. Selah

I'm not sure how long I observed the worship gathering but suddenly, the Trinity stopped dancing. The hand grasp between the Father and the Son dropped. They turned their Faces to the spectating crowd.

The crowd are good to adore the Trinity, BUT we are invited to be their midst. If we enter Their Circle - we will Live and Move and have our Being.

An interpretation:
"We once beheld Them as on a stage, that was worship from afar – that is OLD. Now, we have been invited to enter in to the Union – this is NEW.
You are NEW creatures; your NEW habitation is in ME.

This a New Day:
Worship is to be NEW; no longer OLD!

Your Personal Thoughts/Revelations:

Day 11

Reference:

1 Corinthians 14:14,15 AMPC
[14]For if I pray in an unknown tongue, my spirit by the Holy Spirit within me prays, but ***my mind is unproductive it bears no fruit and helps nobody***
[15]Then what am I to do?...

Benefit:

The speaking in tongues frees you from the prison of self (unproductive mind).

Anecdote:

The question: "Then what am I to do?"
The answer: "Speak in tongues!"

A benefit of speaking in tongues is FREEDOM. Praying in tongues frees the real you from you. Or better said, "allows the real you be defined by God and NOT defined by systems, people, self, circumstances, and/or memories.

Your **New life** is hidden with Christ!

Colossians 3:1-5 APMC
[1]If then you have been raised with Christ [to a new life, thus sharing His resurrection from the dead], aim at *and* seek the [rich, eternal treasures] that are above, where Christ is, seated at the right hand of God.
[2] And set your minds *and* keep them set on what is above (the higher things), not on the things that are on the earth.
[3] For [as far as this world is concerned] you have died, and **your [new, real] life is hidden with Christ in God**.

> [4] **When Christ, Who is our life**, appears, then you also will appear with Him in [the splendor of His] glory.
> [5] So kill (deaden, [a]deprive of power) the evil desire lurking in your members [those animal impulses and all that is earthly in you that is employed in sin]: sexual vice, impurity, sensual appetites, unholy desires, and all greed *and* covetousness, for that is idolatry (the deifying of self and other created things instead of God).

According to Colossians, the 'you' I'm referring to is your id. According to Sigmund Freud, the "**id, ego, and super-ego** are three distinct, yet interacting agents in the psyche of man." It can get crowded in our skulls.

No need to go back to school – Jesus made a (non-confusing) way and told us what to when your Id gets vocal – "Set your mind on things above!"

A practical example, after cramming for exams during finals week in college – I would spend a weekend alone in a hotel room. No phone (only accepting calls from parents), TV unplugged, armed with water, a Christian biography, Bible and a notebook. This was my efforts to pull my mind out of stuff and set my mind on things above. [For my ears, I had some worship songs but mostly filled my ears with the prayers of my spirit (languages unlearned).

What efforts are you willing to do live this New Life?

Speaking in tongues is a way to a new life!

Your Personal Thoughts:

Day 12

Reference: John 7:38 AMPC

38 He who believes in Me as the Scripture has said, from his innermost being shall flow [continuously] springs and rivers of living water.

Benefit:

A lifestyle of speaking in tongues will change the environment around you.

Anecdote:

A lifestyle of speaking in tongues will soak everything around you.

On the first Sunday morning of 2019, I was visiting a small church in Oklahoma City, OK. I arrived a bit early, eyed the front row but opted to sit in the middle section, row 2, aisle. Someone from the choir opened the service. She said, "Turn to your neighbor, look them deep in their eyes, and tell them what you see." I had no neighbor to my right or left, but there were a "set of eyes" on the row in front of me. I moved from my row and sat down in the front row to the right of Donna (the owner of the set of eyes). I introduced myself and proceeded to tell her what I saw. She smiled. After our conversation, the music and the singers started. Normally, I jump up and go for it! One of my former pastors always says,

"Worship is a FULL Contact Sport."

I noticed Donna's cane and she did not rise to sing. Hmmm, it seemed right to remain seated with her. After a couple of songs, I started to speak in tongues. It seemed I was interceding (praying for a specific situation).

Sometimes, I place my hands on my stomach and 'visualize' the John 7 scripture, "... from his belly shall flow rivers..." This time I felt I was to fill up the front area of the sanctuary with my 'flowing river'". So, I kept my eyes closed and continued to pray in tongues. After a song I peeked in the spirit, I could see water up to my ankle and the first step of the stage. A few songs later the water was up to the stage, up to my neck, and rising. I started wondering if I would drown in this 'spiritual water.' The water continued to rise. As it approached my nose, it seemed that I had a choice:

(1) continue to engage the water or
(2) disengage and have a normal Sunday church service.

"Normal is way over-rated" so, I decided to see what was going to happen with all this water. At that moment, the lady at the piano started singing a song about an angel that stirred the waters (read John 5:2-4). According to the scriptures, the one who enter the waters would be healed. As the song continued, a man left the audience, passed through the waters, and mounted the stage. This man was the pastor. He announced, "I've been pastoring for this past year and I'm burned out..." Members of the congregation responded by crossing the waters, mounting the stage, and praying for their pastor.

True enough from my belly (innermost), rivers of living water flowed and a man was restored. You too can release these rivers?

Let the rivers flow!

Your Personal Thoughts/Revelations:

Day 13

Reference:

Acts 19:6 AMPC
[6] And as Paul **laid his hands upon them, the Holy Spirit came on them; and they spoke** in tongues (languages) **and prophesied**.

1 Corinthians 14:1 AMPC
[1] Eagerly pursue and seek to acquire [this] love [make it your aim, your great quest]; and earnestly desire and cultivate the spiritual endowments (gifts) **especially that you prophesy**

Benefit:

Speaking in tongues is another evidence of receiving the Holy Spirit by the laying on of hands

Plus, speaking in tongues can lead to prophesying.

Anecdote:

Speaking in tongues edifies you (builds you) so that you can edify others. It takes being strong in Him, to speak to individuals or crowds.

After I received my 'prayer language' at the Kansas group (re-read starting at page 5), I was diligent to regularly speak in tongues usually at night before bed. Also, when we gathered on Sunday & Wednesday nights, I would speak in tongues during the prayer time. One night after prayer during snack time, I was talking to a friend and a strange-thing-to-me happened: I began to start getting "prophetic words". You may ask, "What are prophetic words?" Let me define them biblically as, "Information that is not from 'flesh and blood but from My Father who is in heaven (Matthew 16:16,17).'

"Simon Peter replied, You are the Christ, the Son of the living God.

Then Jesus answered him, Blessed are you, Simon Bar-Jonah. For flesh and blood have not revealed this to you, but My Father Who is in heaven."

So, my first conscious "heavenly hearing" was, "I think you and your best friend are having a problem." I thought; I would be received like Jesus received Peter. But my female friend denied my prophetic words, "Me and my friend have no problems". I was shocked that I was wrong. I must have heard the words wrong. I walked to the other-side of the room and started having an argument with God. The silent argument got heated but then interrupted. She said, "You know, me and my best friend are having some issues…" I replied, "What, a minute ago you said…"

So, my first prophecy (words from God to help a person) was accurate. There was a bit of a delay, but my friend benefitted from knowing that God was interested in her personal relationship.

Note: as you begin edifying friends, family, and the world with prophecy – remember your Heavenly Father is always correct – people are not the best validators!

Speak in Tongues; Be Bold; and Prophecy!

Your Personal Thoughts/Revelations:

Day 14

Reference: Mark 16:17 AMPC

[17]And these attesting signs will accompany those who believe in My name they will drive out demons; they will speak in new languages.

Benefit:

He who speaks in tongues speaks God's language in perfect "dialect" to YHVH.

Anecdote:

Every child speaks the language of their Father! You are born of God thus be 'normal' and speak the language of God. Remember, "Father knows best". And Father God (Abba) was very active these very proficient language centers:

(1) The Tower of Babel in the land of Shinar (Genesis 11:1-9)

[1]Now the ***whole world had one language and a common speech****.* *[2] As people moved eastward, they found a plain in Shinar and settled there. [3] They said to each other, "Come, let's make bricks and bake them thoroughly." They used brick instead of stone, and tar for mortar. [4] Then they said, "Come, let us build ourselves a city, with a tower that reaches to the heavens, so that we may make a name for ourselves; otherwise we will be scattered over the face of the whole earth." [5] But the LORD came down to see the city and the tower the people were building. [6] The LORD said, "If as one*

people speaking the same language they have begun to do this, then nothing they plan to do will be impossible for them. [7] ***Come, let us go down and confuse their language so they will not understand each other**." * [8] *So the* L*ORD scattered them from there over all the earth, and they stopped building the city.* [9] *That is why it was called Babel—because there the* L*ORD confused the language of the whole world. From there the* L*ORD scattered them over the face of the whole earth.*

(2) <u>The Upper room in Jerusalem</u> <u>(Acts 2:1-4)</u>

[1]*When the day of Pentecost came, they were all together in one place.* [2] *Suddenly a sound like the blowing of a violent wind came from heaven and filled the whole house where they were sitting.* [3] *They saw what seemed to be tongues of fire that separated and came to rest on each of them.* [4] *All of them were filled with the Holy Spirit and* ***<u>began to speak in other languages (tongues) as the Spirit enabled them.</u>***

At the tower of Babel, Abba removed LANGUAGE from the world and in Jerusalem Abba restored LANGUAGE to the world. The language of Babel was meant for evil; the heavenly language is meant for good!

Your Personal Thoughts/Revelations:

Day 15

Reference: 1 Corinthians 14:14 AMPC
[14]For if I pray in an unknown tongue, my spirit by the Holy Spirit within me prays, but my mind is unproductive it bears no fruit and helps nobody.

Benefit:

The act of speaking in tongues requests new resources to be sown into mind.

Anecdote:

Your spirit via speaking tongues is productive - it bears fruit and helps everybody! Speaking in tongues, orders Kingdom-made resources to be downloaded and planted into the natural mind. These 'spiritual resources' revitalize the mind. These spiritual nutrients make that natural mind able to bear fruit. Your mind can be transformed and be restored to it is pre-earth design and function. It can be fruitful as it was originally designed. Just as soil needs to have the correct balance/amounts of minerals, your mind needs to the right resources to function.

The slogan, "The mind is a terrible thing to waste" is a phrase from an '80s commercial. It was referencing the mind being influenced by drugs. **1 Corinthians 14 references the mind being influence by the spirit.** Abba, our heavenly Father, has given us a resource so that our minds can be productive and beneficial to self and others.

A mind based only on facts and experiences and NOT the spirit is a terrible thing to waste. Speaking in tongues allows you "to set your mind on things above." **Colossians 3:2**

> *"And set your minds and keep them set on what is above..."*

Your Personal Thoughts/Revelations:

Day 16

Reference: James 3:7,8 AMPC
[7] For every kind of beast and bird, of reptile and sea animal, can be tamed and has been tamed by human genius (nature).
[8] But the human tongue can be tamed by no man…

Benefit:

He who speaks in tongues actually tames their tongue. Speaking in tongues enhances your ability to live from the inside out.

Anecdote:

Speaking in tongues is not “man-made”; it is Spirit-made. Thus, the tongue is not tamed by “human genius (nature)” but by your new nature that you have in Christ.

We all have problems with language. It’s not your fault; language is comprised of words and words are NOT the best containers. Your native language is not as efficient or effective as images. The language of the King and His Kingdom is FULLY ILLUSTRATED.

> **John 5:19**
> *“…but He is able to do only what He **SEES** the Father doing…”*

The more you speak in tongues the stronger your inner-man becomes. Before you were spirit filled and spoke in tongues, your human reasoning was the sole author of your words. The more you speak in tongues, it gives your inner man new sources of images. Your inner man will begin to produce ‘High Definition” images. You will be like your elder brother, Jesus, and also **SEE** what the Father is doing! **A tamed tongue qualifies a son’s eyes!**

Your Personal Thoughts/Revelations:

Day 17

Reference:

Isaiah 33:17-19 AMPC
[17] Your eyes will see the King in His beauty; your eyes will behold a land of wide distances that stretches afar.
[18] Your mind will meditate on the terror: asking Where is he who counted? Where is he who weighed the tribute? Where is he who counted the towers?
[19] You will see no more the fierce and insolent people, a people of a speech too deep and obscure to be comprehended, of a strange and stammering tongue that you cannot understand.

Benefit:

Speaking tongues also helps the mind not to "meditate on the terror" and then synchronizes the mind and the eyes of your heart to **SEE the King and His Kingdom!"**

Anecdote:

I believe the 'stammering tongue' is an Old Testament reference for the New Testament, speaking in tongues. To the natural man, speaking tongues is "too deep and obscure to be comprehended..." Speaking in tongues does more than meets the eye; it causes your eyes to see **the King in His beauty!"**

In our congregation, there was an older lady who would go forward during worship, take the microphone and share a 'stammering tongue'. Well the first few times she would do it, I was amazed at her boldness and confidence. I was spirit-filled but have never spoken in tongues before a group. I was even more amazed when she would interpret the 'stammer tongue'.

But my awe soon turned to distain. Every time she would go forward she would stammer the same 'obscure, comprehendible', short phrase. Then, she would say, "God loves you" and walk back up the aisle to her backrow seat.

I'm not sure how often she did it, but it began to grate on me. I kept hoping that 'stammering phrase' would change but "Nope." I kept waiting for the church leadership to correct her or stop her but "Nope." According to my mind, her tongues were fake, and she was just doing it for personal attention. I was firm with my belief until one Friday night.

I grew up using the TV as background noise. So, it was not unusual for me to be in my bedroom while the TV is blaring in the living room. I think I was getting ready to go to a movie or something. I step out the shower, dry off, put on deodorant, and then I hear it. I heard the church lady's stammering tongue. I froze. It was her tongue except it was not a short phrase. I darted to the TV room to see & hear several men - speaking in a 'very-familiar-to-me' tongue. OMG, the church lady was "legit", and I was corrected.

Your Personal Thoughts/Revelations:

Day 18

Reference: 1 Corinthians 14:15 AMPC
[15] **I will** pray with the Spirit, and **I will** pray with the understanding.

Benefit:

Praying with the spirit adds another tool to a believer's arsenal.

Anecdote:

Every citizen should be armed and dangerous, a dual-threat. Praying with the spirit (aka speaking to Abba in a foreign tongue) and praying with the understanding (aka speaking to Abba in your native tongue).

All the "I willers" become a powerful double threat! An "I willer" is someone in active, vital relationship with Abba. This person makes This Relationship paramount and knows (experiences) the **ABUNDANT** life promised by our elder brother, Yeshua.

John 10:10 AMPC
...I came that they may have and enjoy life, and have it in ABUNDANCE (to the full, till it overflows).

The Trinity have been planning this before time, before *bereishit* (the beginning). They have had you in mind, in heart, actually in spirit. It's Their **great pleasure** to give.

Luke 12:32 AMPC
...for it is your Father's good ***PLEASURE*** *to give you the kingdom!*

Your Personal Thoughts/Revelations:

Day 19

Reference: 1 Corinthians 14:1 Message

[1]Go after a life of love as if your life depended on it – because it does. Give yourselves to the gifts that God gives you.

Benefit:

He who speaks in tongues opens the door to the miraculous and gains access to other spiritual gifts.

Anecdote:

John 10:9 AMPC
I am the Door; anyone who enters in through Me will live. He will come in and he will go out and find pasture.

For God so loved the world He gave a "door" (aka His only begotten Son). Doors and Jesus are to be used. The Godhead specializes in making "ways" (aka doors). God's doors lead to LIFE. This is their way: They initiate. **Will you respond?** The issue is the response. Speaking in tongues is a response that opens the door.

These open doors manifest in various ways: memories, unique encounters with people, places, or things. In 2010, I was given an open door in the form of a book, "The Ecstasy of Loving God," by John Crowder. I engaged the door and learned that I could "love God as much as He loved me." Going through that door was 'future shaping'. The 1st chapter of that book reignited or better said, ignited my relationship with LIFE.

Those open doors gave access to:
"Revelation is borne from relationship; divine revelation is born from divine relationship!"

Your Personal Thoughts/Revelations:

Day 20

Reference:

1 Corinthians 14:2 AMPC
[2]For one who speaks in an unknown tongue speaks not to men but to God, for no one understands or catches his meaning, because in the Holy Spirit he utters secret truths and hidden things not obvious to the understanding.

Benefit:

Speaking in tongues leads to understanding His secret truths and hidden things (sod)

Anecdote:

In Hebrew hermeneutics, "sod" is the deep, hidden, layered meanings in the scriptures. We can pursue God naturally or spiritually. I recommend a spiritual pursuit. On this planet and under multiple systems, we have been taught to lean towards the natural. If you wish to grow, you will need to **rebel** against the world system, the religious system, and the natural system.
The mysteries revealed are the mysteries that seal the deal and pave the way… His ways lead to maturity and to LIFE its self.

Recently, some mysteries from Genesis Chapter 5 were revealed:

(a) There was no time in the garden;
(b) When Adam departed the garden, they became subject to time;
(c) This new force, time, was new to Adam;
(d) This Time-force was stronger than expected;
(e) Time had the ability to "lie, deceive, & bind"
(f) The first six generations believed the lie
(g) Only Enoch escaped the web of lies to walk with God

Your Personal Thoughts/Revelations:

Day 21

Reference: Romans 8:26 AMPC

[26]So too the [Holy] Spirit comes to our aid and bears us up in our weakness; for we do not know **what prayer to offer nor how to offer it worthily as we ought**, but the Spirit Himself goes to meet our supplication and pleads in our behalf with unspeakable yearnings and groanings too deep for utterance.

Benefit:

He who speaks in tongues has means to effective, perfect intercession

Anecdote:

Most people do not pray effectively; thus, their prayers are not answered. Unanswered prayer leads some people to be angry with God. Effective refers to the CORRECT type of prayer. Most people believe if you add the (magic words) "in Jesus Name" and/or "Amen" to your prayer then it will be answered. Following that doctrine, will lead you to even more frustration.

> **Ephesians 6:18 AMPC**
> Pray at all times in the Spirit… interceding in behalf of all the saints.

I had to move to Sweden, read a book, spend nine months in bible school, and attend prayer school to learn there are many diverse types of prayer. You don't need a passport or more information to pray effectively. You do need to be aided. Let me save you time and introduce you to the "Prayer Consultant". He always knows "**what prayer to offer and how to offer it worthily…**" (Rom. 8:26)

Your Personal Thoughts/Revelations:

Day 22

Reference: Ephesians 5:18 AMPC
[18]And do not get drunk with wine, for that is debauchery; but ever be filled and stimulated with the [Holy] Spirit.

Benefit:

Speaking in tongues keeps you filled with the Spirit. We are like helium (spirit) filled balloons, without remaining full we will never reach great heights!

Anecdote:

Hebrews 12:1 AMPC
...let us strip off *and* **throw aside every encumbrance (unnecessary weight)** and that sin which so readily (deftly and cleverly) clings to *and* entangles us, and let us run with patient endurance *and* steady *and* active persistence the appointed course of the race that is set before us.

There have been times when I've stumbled and fallen during my "race". I have found that regular, consistent, long periods of speaking in tongues has kept me filled. It has caused me to "**throw aside every encumbrance (unnecessary weight)**" unresolvable issues.

I heard a long time ago that our earthen vessels are porous; they leak. Speaking in tongues keeps me filled, inflated so I can continue to race not at earthly standards but the ability to run at heaven's pace.

Your Personal Thoughts/Revelations:

Day 23

Reference: Ephesians 6:18 AMPC

[18] Pray at all times (on every occasion, in every season) in the Spirit, with all [manner of] prayer and entreaty. To that end keep alert and watch with strong purpose *and* perseverance, interceding in behalf of all the saints (God's consecrated people).

Benefit:

Speaking tongues leads to unrestrained prayer.

Anecdote:

When you are fluent in your prayer language(s), your prayers take you outside time-space. Your fluent tongues are NOT limited by time or space. I'm learning that sons of God are not limited. The more you pray in tongues, the more you live. The more you live "the life"; the more opportunities you acquire in which you can choose to BELIEVE.

John 6:29 (AMPC)

[29] Jesus replied, This is the work (service) that God asks of you: **that you BELIEVE** in the One Whom He has sent [that you cleave to, trust, rely on, and have faith in His Messenger].

Yeshua said in **Mark 11:24**, “When you pray, believe…” Nothing is more important than your ability to believe. Belief is another gift from our Father.

As I’ve unwrapped and learned to play with this gift, everything changes! I can definitively say, this and my other books were born from my thousands of hours of tongues.

> **Mark 9:23 (AMPC)**
> 23 And Jesus said, [You say to Me], If You can do anything? [Why,] all things can be (are possible) to him who believes!

*Bonus **Benefit**: praying and/or singing in tongues will enhance your current creativity or provide creativity to those who need it □

It’s time to explore the benefits of unrestrained prayer!

Your Personal Thoughts/Revelations:

Day 24

Reference: Galatians 6:8,9 AMPC

[8] Whoever sows to please their flesh, from the flesh will reap destruction; ***whoever sows to please the Spirit, from the Spirit will reap*** *eternal life.*
[9] Let us not become weary in doing good, for at the proper time we will reap a harvest if we do not give up.

Benefit:

Speaking in tongues allows you to sow to please the Spirit

Anecdote:

Speaking in tongues is most definitely sowing to please the Spirit and this is an awesome mutual benefit. It's amazing that we have the ability to bring pleasure to the Almighty God. For many decades I didn't care about pleasing Him since I was busy working for Him. My years in sports had trained me to perform for my audiences and to seek the approval of my coaches. Those habits followed me into my kingdom life.

1 John 4:19 AMPC
We love Him, because He first loved us.

But, once I started to receive His LOVE; I was then motivated to pursue Him. After a while, I captured my pursuit and vital union began.

In **UNION**, human habits and traits are replaced with divine attributes.

UNION is the path to the **GLORY**!

Your Personal Thoughts/Revelations:

Day 25

Reference: Hebrews 11:3 AMPC

[3]By faith we understand that the worlds [during the successive ages] were framed (fashioned, put in order, and equipped for their intended purpose) by the word of God, so that what we see was not made out of things which are visible.

Benefit:

He who speaks in tongues speaks mysteries, these (tongue) words frame your future

Anecdote:

Consistent, frequent, fluent, persistent, intentional tongues will construct, fashion, put in order, and equip you and your worlds for their intended Kingdom purpose!

Your future (the world that comes after today) is in your mouth!

You will begin to partner, co-create with your Heavenly Father. You will witness that which we see with our natural eyes is not fashioned from things which are visible.

Ephesians 2:10 AMPC

[10] For we are God's [own] handiwork (His workmanship), recreated in Christ Jesus, [born anew] that we may do those good works which God predestined (planned beforehand) for us [taking paths which He prepared ahead of time], that we should walk in them [living the good life which He prearranged and made ready for us to live].

Your Personal Thoughts/Revelations:

Day 26

Reference: Revelation 3:20 AMPC

[20] Behold, I stand at the door and knock; if anyone hears *and* listens to *and* heeds My voice and opens the door, I will come in to him and will eat with him, and he [will eat] with Me.

Benefit:

Speaking in tongues opens doors, that mere man can see or open!

Anecdote:

John 14:2 AMPC

[2]In My Father's house there are many dwelling places (homes). If it were not so, I would have told you, for I am going away to prepare a place for you.

"Many dwelling places" means many doors! Many doors mean many ways to mature. I believe, Father knows best and we are His workmanship created to walk in the good works that He prearrange and made ready for us to prosper from.

John 10:33 AMPC

[33]The Jews replied, We are not going to stone You for a good act, but for blasphemy, because You, a mere man, make Yourself [out to be] God.

A mere man has no chance without divine help. God so loved the world that He has provided a divine life line.

Galatians 4:1,2 AMPC
[1]Now what I mean is that as long as the inheritor (heir) is a child and under age, he does not differ from a slave, although he is the master of all the estate;
[2]But he (heir) is under guardians and administrators or trustees until the date fixed by his father.

I believe the "guardians" are *angels (Matt. 4:11); the "administrators" are the **seven spirits of God (2 Chronicles 16:9 and Revelation 5:6); and the "trustees" are from the church of the Firstborn (Hebrews 12:23).

In September 2018, the Father re-introduced me to the spirit of Might. Here is a little of what I was told:

1. "You will walk with the spirit of Might this year (5779).
2. He will help you believe to new levels of possibilities!
3. What's possible is directly related to the depth of intimacy you have with the Pre-eminent Authority in your reality."

So, I'm under an administrator (the spirit of Might) until 'the date fixed by the (heavenly) Father'. I was impressed when I met the individual seven spirits. Now, I'm learning from one of them.

**See the book: "A Mystical Introduction to Angels"*
***See the book: "An Introduction to the Seven Spirits of God"*

Your Personal Thoughts/Revelations:

Day 27

Reference: I Corinthians 14:6 Mirror
[6]Imagine how confusing it would be if I visit you and all I do is impress you with **my spirituality** by speaking in tongues; how could I possibly benefit you unless I speak with revelation insight and inspired prophetic instruction.

Benefit:

Speaking in tongues expands your spirituality

Anecdote:

1 Corinthians 2:14 (AMPC)
[14] But the natural, nonspiritual man does not accept *or* welcome *or* admit into his heart the gifts *and* teachings *and* revelations of the Spirit of God, for they are folly to him; and he is incapable of knowing them [of progressively recognizing, understanding, and becoming better acquainted with them] because they are **spiritually discerned** *and* estimated *and* appreciated.

Slowly, re-read the above again.
"Natural" is way over rated. Speaking in tongues makes you spiritual by causing you to become "spiritually discerning". Only a spiritual man can accept the teachings *and* revelations of the Spirit of God; a spiritual man is capable of **KNOWING** all spiritual matters and operations.

Your Personal Thoughts/Revelations:

Day 28

Reference: 1 Corinthians 14:22 AMPC

[22]Thus [unknown] tongues are meant for a [supernatural] sign, not for believers but for unbelievers…

Benefit:

Speaking in tongues is a sign to unbelievers (believing, doubters)

Anecdote:

Speaking in tongues is a means of "evangelism" to unbelievers. Understand the definition of this breed of unbeliever. Now, only the Spirit will lead you to this 'type' of unbeliever (believing, doubters) and utilize His supernatural strategy. It was very effective in the book of Acts chapter 2.

Acts 2:4-11 (NIV)

[4] All of them were filled with the Holy Spirit and began to speak in other tongues as the Spirit enabled them.

[5] Now there were staying in Jerusalem God-fearing Jews from every nation under heaven.

[6] When they heard this sound, a crowd came together in bewilderment, because each one heard their own language being spoken.

[7] Utterly amazed, they asked: "Aren't all these who are speaking Galileans?

[8] Then how is it that each of us hears them in our native language?
[9] Parthians, Medes and Elamites; residents of Mesopotamia, Judea and Cappadocia, Pontus and Asia,
[10] Phrygia and Pamphylia, Egypt and the parts of Libya near Cyrene; visitors from Rome
[11] (both Jews and converts to Judaism); Cretans and Arabs—we hear them declaring the wonders of God in our own tongues!"

Every strategy initiated by the Holy Spirit is exceedingly efficient and successful!

Romans 8:14 (KJV)
[14] For as many as are led by the Spirit of God, they are the sons of God.

We should stop thinking 'we' are so smart and just **follow The Leader**!

Being enable by the Spirit is your (new) birthright. It is time to know and exercise your rights.

Exercise daily; Speak in tongues daily!

Galatians 5:18 (KJV)
[18] But if ye be led of the Spirit, ye are not under the law.

Your Personal Thoughts/Revelations:

Day 29

Reference: Mark 16:17 NIV

[17] And these signs will accompany those who believe: In My Name they will drive out demons; <u>they will speak in new tongues</u>…

Benefit:

Speaking in tongues is a sign that accompanies believers; it is also an evidence of being baptized in the Holy Spirit.

Anecdote:

Doubters do not speak in tongues. **Every believer speaks in tongues.** This is true for at least two reasons:

(1) Because Father says so and
(2) All things are possible for believers.

I can hear your thoughts across time-space, "I know many 'believers' who don't speak in tongues; even some 'believers' still despise speaking in tongues…" If you continue and take those thoughts to throne of grace you will have some excellent interactions/conversations with Abba.

Jesus said, "Man shall not live by bread alone but by every word that proceeds from the mouth of God (Matthew 4:4)." Faith comes by hearing and hearing from a <u>Father-son-believing relationship</u>.

Everyone in vital union with their Heavenly Father will be like Him. Faith works by LOVE. God is LOVE. **Love never fails!** In Him, doubters will not only see the sign, but they will become the sign.

Resistance is futile!

Your Personal Thoughts/Revelations:

Day 30

Reference: John 7:38,39 AMPC

[38]He who believes in Me [who cleaves to *and* trusts in *and* relies on Me] as the Scripture has said, From his innermost being shall flow [continuously] springs *and* rivers of living water.
[39]But He was speaking here of the Spirit, Whom those who believed in Him were afterward to receive…

Benefit:

Your prayer language will give you the ability to terraform EVERYTHING around you by the LIVing water

Anecdote:

Terraforming, eroding, manifesting, transfiguring – what do these words have in common? Well other than ending with "ing", they all relate to creation.

- Natural water erodes the natural.
- Living water supports terraforming!
- Living water supports manifesting!
- Living water supports transfiguring!

Genesis 2:10 (AMPC)
[10] Now a river went out of Eden to water the garden; and from there it divided and became four [river] heads.

Psalm 46:4 (AMPC)

[4] There is a river whose streams shall make glad the city of God, the holy place of the tabernacles of the Most High.

Mighty rushing waters flowing from your belly - those waters "make glad the city of God!" Like all living waters, they bring life to where they flow!

The first time I consciously saw these waters flow was in a public restaurant. I left church with a new visitor and we went to Wendy's for an after-service meal. The place was packed. We got trays of food and made our way to the only two seats in the center of the room. We sat with two other hungry people.

I ate.

The new visitor began to speak; the river began to flow.

Something was happening in our packed restaurant. I look up from my burger and the two people at our table were gone. Two bites later, the table to my right was empty. A few fries later, the table in front of me was empty. The new visitor continued speaking. He was talking about stuff that God was doing in the earth.

I finished my meal, but the man was not done sharing 'God tales'. Now all the surrounding tables were empty. This was very odd since all the other tables were full. No one sat in those tables until we left.

Ezekiel 47:1-12 AMPC

47 Then he [my guide] brought me again to the door of the house [of the Lord—the temple], and behold, **waters issued out from under the threshold of the temple** toward the east, for the front of the temple was toward the east; and the waters came down from under, from the right side of the temple, on the south side of the altar.

[2] Then he brought me out by way of the north gate and led me around outside to the outer gate by the way that faces east, and behold, waters were running out on the right side.

[3] And when the man went on eastward with the measuring line in his hand, he measured a thousand cubits, and he caused me to pass through the waters, waters that were ankle-deep.

[4] Again he measured a thousand cubits and caused me to pass through the waters, waters that reached to the knees. Again, he measured a thousand cubits and caused me to pass through the waters, waters that reached to the loins.

[5] Afterward he measured a thousand, and it was a river that I could not pass through,

for the waters had risen, waters to swim in, a river that could not be passed over *or* through.

6 And he said to me, Son of man, have you seen this? Then he led me and caused me to return to the bank of the river.

7 Now when I had returned, behold, on the bank of the river were very many trees on the one side and on the other.

8 Then he said to me, These waters pour out toward the eastern region and go down into the Arabah (the Jordan Valley) and on into the Dead Sea. And when they shall enter into the sea [the sea of putrid waters], the waters shall be healed *and* made fresh.

9 And wherever the double river shall go, every living creature which swarms shall live. And there shall be a very great number of fish, because these waters go there that [the waters of the sea] may be healed *and* made fresh; and **everything shall live wherever the river goes.**

10 The fishermen shall stand on [the banks of the Dead Sea]; from Engedi even to Eneglaim shall be a place to spread nets; their fish shall be of very many kinds, as the fish of the Great *or* Mediterranean Sea.

[12] And on the banks of the river on both its sides, there shall grow all kinds of trees for food; their leaf shall not fade nor shall their fruit fail [to meet the demand]. Each tree shall bring forth new fruit every month, [these supernatural qualities being] because their waters came from out of the sanctuary. And their fruit shall be for food and their leaves for healing.

Many wondered how Mr. Donald Trump became America's 45th sitting President. I believe it was from the river released from David's Tent, a place of 24-hour worship. Before the 2016 election, hundreds of days & nights of worship had been completed. I believe the river washed away the old and made room for President Trump.

Ephesians 6:10 (AMPC)

[10] In conclusion, be strong in the Lord [be empowered through your union with Him]; draw your strength from Him [that strength which His boundless might provides].

A truth, a promise: in the beginning of 5779 (Fall 2018), two rivers began to merge. We are invited to experience the union of these two Great rivers of "empowerment". There is much LIFE in these relationships:

1. River of relationship with Abba (Father)
2. River of relationship with His Might

Your Personal Thoughts/Revelations:

Day 31

Reference: 1 Corinthians 14:18 AMPC
[18]I thank God that I speak in tongues (languages) more than any of you or all of you put together;

Benefit:

Frequent speaking in tongues leads to mastery of spiritual operations

Anecdote:

1 Corinthians 12:1 KJV
Now concerning **spirituals** brethren, I would not have you ignorant

In some translations, "spirituals" has been translated as 'spiritual gifts'. "Spirituals" is not limited to your understanding or a man's translation.

History suggests that kings needed to speak the languages of the people they ruled; a king needed to know seventy, all the languages of the known world. The King of kings has given you access to the only true universal language, a heavenly language.

Let us go from Kings to Masters. In this modern era, some (see Google) have estimated that it takes 10,000 hours to master something. I believe the Apostle Paul had this in mind when he said, "I speak in tongues more than any of you ..." He was seeking and achieved mastery of spirituals by speaking in tongues more than his peers. The Apostle gave us a standard, "speak in tongues more than your friends (and enemies). **When you achieve mastery, you are NO LONGER IGNORANT of spiritual operations**, activities, matters in (or out of) our Fathers Kingdom!

Your Personal Thoughts/Revelations:

"Only one who devotes himself to a cause with his whole strength and soul can be a true master. For this reason mastery demands all of a person" -- Albert Einstein

List of Benefits

Day	Benefits	Reference
1	Speaking in tongues allows you to be biblical; a true doer of the word!	1 Cor.14: 39
2	You get to by-pass "the line" and speak directly to the Source.	1 Cor.14: 2
3	A. Speaking in tongues allows one to engage in His Kingdom as a citizen and as a son of the King. B. Speaking in tongues cause you to receive the "mind of Christ".	1 Cor.14: 2
4	If you speak in tongues, you become **strong** in spirit.	1 Cor.14: 4,5
5	Speaking in tongues prepares your inner man for modifications	1 Cor.14: 4
6	Speaking in tongues can and will build up your (vital) faith.	Jude 20
7	A. Speaking in tongues triggers Love in you and out of you! B. Also, speaking in tongues supports the bonding of host and the Divine.	Jude 21
8	A. Speaking in tongues causes the brain to become familiar with mysteries. B. Speaking in tongues opens the mind to mysteries.	1 Cor.14: 2
9	He who speaks in tongues conditions his mind as a King.	1 Cor. 14:14
10	When you choose to speak in tongues, you create 'the occasion' and you open opportunities for you and others to be a blessing.	Gal. 6:10

Day	Benefits (continued)	Reference
11	The speaking in tongues frees you from the prison of self.	1 Cor. 14:14,15
12	A lifestyle of speaking in tongues will change the environment around you.	John 7:38
13	A. Evidence of receiving the Holy Spirit by the laying on of hands B. Plus, speaking in tongues can lead to prophesying.	Acts 19:6
14	He who speaks in tongues speaks God's language in perfect "dialect" to YHVH.	Mk. 16:17
15	The act of speaking in tongues requests new resources to be sown into mind.	1 Cor 14:14 Col 3:2
16	A. He who speaks in tongues tames their natural tongue. B. Speaking in tongues enhances your ability to live from the inside out.	James 3:7,8
17	A. Speaking tongues also helps the mind not to "meditate on the terror" and B. then synchronizes the mind and the eyes of your heart to see	Is. 33:17-19
18	Praying with the spirit adds another tool to a believer's arsenal.	1 Cor.14: 15
19	A. He who speaks in tongues opens the door to the miraculous and B. Also gains access to other spiritual gifts	1 Cor.14: 1

Day	Benefits (continued)	Reference
20	Speaking in tongues leads to understanding secret truths and hidden things (Hebrew: sod)	1 Cor.14: 2
21	He who speaks in tongues has means to effective, perfect intercession	Rom. 8:26
22	Speaking in tongues keeps you filled with the Spirit	Eph. 5:18
23	A. Speaking tongues leads to unrestrained prayer B. Praying and/or singing in tongues will enhance your current creativity or provide creativity to those who need it	Eph. 6:18
24	Speaking in tongues allows you to sow to please the Spirit	Gal. 6:8,9
25	He who speaks in tongues speaks mysteries, these (tongue) words frame your future	Heb. 11:3
26	Speaking in tongues opens doors, that no man can see or open!	Rev. 3:20
27	Speaking in tongues expands your spirituality	1 Cor.14: 6
28	Speaking in tongues is a sign to unbelievers (believing, doubters)	1 Cor.14: 22
29	A. Speaking in tongues is a sign that accompanies believers; B. it is also an evidence of being baptized in the Holy Spirit.	Mark 16:17

Day	Benefits (continued)	Reference
30	Your prayer language will give you the ability to terraform EVERYTHING around you	John 7:38,39
31	Leads to mastery of spirituals, spiritual operations	1 Cor. 14:18

#	Other Benefits Don't stop now you should be adding to your list)	Reference
1		
2		
3		
4		
5		
6		
7		
8		
9		
10		
	Watch and learn from this video: https://youtu.be/NZbQBajYnEc	YouTube

1 Corinthians 14 (AMPC)

1 Eagerly pursue *and* seek to acquire [this] love [make it your aim, your great quest]; and earnestly desire *and* cultivate the spiritual endowments (gifts), especially that you may prophesy ([a]interpret the divine will and purpose in inspired preaching and teaching).

2 For one who speaks in an [unknown] tongue speaks not to men but to God, for no one understands *or* catches his meaning, because in the [Holy] Spirit he utters secret truths *and* hidden things [not obvious to the understanding].

3 But [on the other hand], the one who prophesies [who [b]interprets the divine will and purpose in inspired preaching and teaching] speaks to men for their upbuilding *and* constructive spiritual progress and encouragement and consolation.

4 He who speaks in a [strange] tongue edifies *and* improves himself, but he who prophesies [[c]interpreting the divine will and purpose and teaching with inspiration] edifies *and* improves the church *and* promotes growth [in Christian wisdom, piety, holiness, and happiness].

5 Now I wish that you might all speak in [unknown] tongues, but more especially [I want you] to prophesy (to be inspired to preach and interpret the divine will and purpose). He who prophesies [who is inspired to preach and teach] is greater (more useful and more important) than he who speaks in [unknown] tongues, unless he should interpret [what he says], so that the church may be edified *and* receive good [from it].

6 Now, brethren, if I come to you speaking in [unknown] tongues, how shall I make it to your advantage unless I speak to you either in revelation (disclosure of God's will to man) in knowledge or in prophecy or in instruction?

[7] If even inanimate musical instruments, such as the flute or the harp, do not give distinct notes, how will anyone [listening] know *or* understand what is played?

[8] And if the war bugle gives an uncertain (indistinct) call, who will prepare for battle?

[9] Just so it is with you; if you in the [unknown] tongue speak words that are not intelligible, how will anyone understand what you are saying? For you will be talking into empty space!

[10] There are, I suppose, all these many [to us unknown] tongues in the world [somewhere], and none is destitute of [its own power of] expression *and* meaning.

[11] But if I do not know the force *and* significance of the speech (language), I shall seem to be a foreigner to the one who speaks [to me], and the speaker who addresses [me] will seem a foreigner to me.

[12] So it is with yourselves; since you are so eager *and* ambitious to possess spiritual endowments *and* manifestations of the [Holy] Spirit, [concentrate on] striving to excel *and* to abound [in them] in ways that will build up the church.

[13] Therefore, the person who speaks in an [unknown] tongue should pray [for the power] to interpret *and* explain what he says.

[14] For if I pray in an [unknown] tongue, my spirit [by the [d] Holy Spirit within me] prays, but my mind is unproductive [it bears no fruit and helps nobody].

[15] Then what am I to do? I will pray with my spirit [by the [e] Holy Spirit that is within me], but I will also pray [intelligently] with my mind *and* understanding; I will sing with my spirit [by the Holy Spirit that is within me], but I will sing [intelligently] with my mind *and* understanding also.

[16]Otherwise, if you bless *and* render thanks with [your] spirit [[f]thoroughly aroused by the Holy Spirit], how can anyone in the position of an outsider *or* he who is not gifted with [interpreting of unknown] tongues, say the Amen to your thanksgiving, since he does not know what you are saying?

[17]To be sure, you may give thanks well (nobly), but the bystander is not edified [it does him no good].

[18]I thank God that I speak in [strange] tongues (languages) more than any of you *or* all of you put together;

[19]Nevertheless, in public worship, I would rather say five words with my understanding *and* intelligently in order to instruct others, than ten thousand words in a [strange] tongue (language).

[20]Brethren, do not be children [immature] in your thinking; continue to be babes in [matters of] evil, but in your minds be mature [men].

[21]It is written in the Law, By men of strange languages *and* by the lips of foreigners will I speak to this people, and not even then will they listen to Me, says the Lord.

[22]Thus [unknown] tongues are meant for a [supernatural] sign, not for believers but for unbelievers [on the point of believing], while prophecy (inspired preaching and teaching, interpreting the divine will and purpose) is not for unbelievers [on the point of believing] but for believers.

[23]Therefore, if the whole church assembles and all of you speak in [unknown] tongues, and the ungifted *and* uninitiated or unbelievers come in, will they not say that you are demented?

[24]But if all prophesy [giving inspired testimony and interpreting the divine will and purpose] and an unbeliever or untaught outsider comes in, he is told of his sin *and* reproved *and* convicted *and* convinced by all, and his defects *and* needs are examined (estimated, determined) *and* he is called to account by all,

[25] The secrets of his heart are laid bare; and so, falling on [his] face, he will worship God, declaring that God is among you in very truth.

[26] What then, brethren, is [the right course]? When you meet together, each one has a hymn, a teaching, a disclosure of special knowledge *or* information, an utterance in a [strange] tongue, or an interpretation of it. [But] let everything be constructive *and* edifying *and* for the good of all.

[27] If some speak in a [strange] tongue, let the number be limited to two or at the most three, and each one [taking his] turn, and let one interpret *and* explain [what is said].

[28] But if there is no one to do the interpreting, let each of them keep still in church and talk to himself and to God.

[29] So let two or three prophets speak [those inspired to preach or teach], while the rest pay attention *and* weigh *and* discern what is said.

[30] But if an inspired revelation comes to another who is sitting by, then let the first one be silent.

[31] For in this way you can give testimony [prophesying and thus interpreting the divine will and purpose] one by one, so that all may be instructed and all may be stimulated *and* encouraged;

[32] For the spirits of the prophets (the speakers in tongues) are under the speaker's control [and subject to being silenced as may be necessary],

[33] For He [Who is the source of their prophesying] is not a God of confusion *and* disorder but of peace *and* order. As [is the practice] in all the churches of the saints (God's people),

[34] The women should keep quiet in the churches, for they are not authorized to speak, but should take a secondary *and* subordinate place, just as the Law also says.

[35] But if there is anything they want to learn, they should ask their own husbands at home, for it is disgraceful for a woman to talk in church [[a]for her to usurp and exercise authority over men in the church].

[36] What! Did the word of the Lord originate with you [Corinthians], or has it reached only you?

[37] If anyone thinks *and* claims that he is a prophet [filled with and governed by the Holy Spirit of God and inspired to interpret the divine will and purpose in preaching or teaching] or has any other spiritual endowment, let him understand (recognize and acknowledge) that what I am writing to you is a command of the Lord.

[38] But if anyone disregards *or* does not recognize [[b]that it is a command of the Lord], he is disregarded *and* not recognized [he is [c]one whom God knows not].

[39] So [to conclude], my brethren, earnestly desire *and* set your hearts on prophesying (on being inspired to preach and teach and to interpret God's will and purpose), and do not forbid *or* hinder speaking in [unknown] tongues.

[40] But all things should be done with regard to decency *and* propriety and in an orderly fashion.

Final Word

Ephesians 6:10
[10] In conclusion, be strong in the Lord [be empowered through your union with Him]; draw your strength from Him [that strength which His boundless might provides].

Years ago, I think in the Spring of 1984, I traveled from my town to a weekly bible study in Kansas City. The pastor of that church had created a one-page flyer entitled, "22 Scriptural Benefits of Speaking in Tongues". It was on the back table of the sanctuary and the price was right, FREE. I grabbed a couple and put them in my bible.

The list of benefits did nothing for me until I tested them. I hope you will do likewise with this book. Test my claims!

Galatians 6:9 (AMPC)
[9] Let us not become weary in doing good, for at the proper time we will reap a harvest if we do not give up.

You want to be STRONG in the Lord? You want stop getting weary in doing good? Do you want to OVERCOME weariness and establish goodness? The answer is simple: follow the leading, promptings of the Spirit and speak in your heavenly language.

Get off your butt! Enter into the arena of life! See if He is the AWESOME GOD. This journey will not disappoint. It is the journey of a lifetime.

You can know Him via experience and your LIFE as you know it will become A LIFE as HE knows it.

My desire is
you will say like
me & the apostle Paul,
"I speak in tongues more than you all..."

Acts 13:36 (AMPC)
For David, after he had served God's will and purpose and counsel in his own generation..."

Is this a key or guidance to the path of becoming the "one" in this generation?

Could praying in tongues be you serving God's will and purpose and counsel?

In conclusion, engage, engage more, and engage yet more!

Speak the language of Kings!

Contact me at ***1newmystic@gmail.com***

Or

at **The Ekklesia Uprising** ***[http://ekklesiauprising.org/]***

(available for conferences, meetings, & mentoring)

Additional Notes

NOTES

NOTES

Made in the USA
Columbia, SC
15 February 2023